RESHAPE YOUR HABITS

BUILD GOOD HABITS

&

BREAK BAD HABITS

S.O. AYOOLA

TABLE OF CONTENTS

PREFACE

The Power of Habits

The Habitual Life

Imagine waking up in the morning and effortlessly going through your routine: you brush your teeth, make a healthy breakfast, exercise for thirty minutes, and then tackle the day's tasks with unparalleled focus and productivity. You're not struggling to make these choices; they've become automatic, ingrained in your daily life.

Now, contrast that with a different scenario: you hit the snooze button multiple times, skip breakfast, reach for your phone, and dive into a sea of distractions. You procrastinate on your important tasks and find yourself overwhelmed by the end of the day. It's as if you're on autopilot, but this time, you're heading towards chaos and unproductivity.

These two scenarios illustrate the immense influence of habits on our lives. Habits are the invisible forces that shape our daily routines, our behaviors, and, ultimately, our destinies. They are the silent architects of our existence, constructing the life we lead, whether we realize it or not.

The Habitual Mind

Our brains are wired for habits. They are, in fact, a testament to the incredible efficiency of our neural networks. When we repeatedly perform an action in response to a specific cue, our brain strives to automate it. This automation is the foundation of habits. It allows our brains to conserve energy and streamline decision-making.

Consider the act of driving a car. When you first learn to drive, every action demands your full attention: shifting gears, applying brakes, checking mirrors, and following traffic rules. But as you gain experience, these actions become second nature. You can have a conversation while driving without consciously thinking about every maneuver. That's the power of habit at work.

Habits are not just limited to mundane activities like brushing your teeth or tying your shoelaces; they extend to every aspect of your life. From your morning routine to your work habits, from the way you interact with others to your health and fitness choices, habits play a pivotal role in determining your quality of life.

The Habitual Society

Zoom out for a moment and look at society as a whole. It, too, is a product of collective habits. The way people interact, the culture they cultivate, and the systems they create are all influenced by habitual behaviors.

Consider the daily habits of millions of people in a city: commuting to work, shopping, eating out, and engaging in leisure activities. These habits shape urban landscapes, transportation systems, and the economy. Our cities are the physical manifestation of societal habits.

On a broader scale, consider the habits that underpin cultural norms, political ideologies, and global trends. The way we approach education, the environment, or technology reflects the collective habits of societies and nations. The world we live in today, with all its complexities and challenges, is a result of countless individual and collective habits.

The Habitual Quest

Given the profound influence of habits, it's crucial to recognize that they are not inherently good or bad. Habits are tools that can either empower us or lead us astray, depending on how we wield them. This book is about harnessing the power of habits to reshape your life for the better.

Whether you aim to become healthier, more productive, or more fulfilled, the journey begins with understanding, cultivating, and transforming your habits. In these pages, we'll explore the science behind habits, the psychology that governs them, and the strategies to cultivate good habits and break free from bad ones.

Reshaping your habits is not a simple task; it's a profound and ongoing journey. It requires self-awareness, discipline, and a deep understanding of how habits are formed and sustained. But the rewards are immense—a life where your desired behaviors become second nature, where you move closer to your goals with each passing day, and where you become the architect of your own destiny.

Navigating the Journey

In the following chapters, we will delve into the fascinating world of habits. We'll begin by dissecting the mechanics of habits, exploring the neurological processes that govern them, and unveiling the habit loop—the cornerstone of habit formation. Understanding this loop will be your first step towards reshaping your habits.

With this foundation in place, we'll embark on a comprehensive exploration of the habits that shape different facets of your life. From health and wellness to productivity and relationships, we'll uncover the habits that hold the keys to a better, more fulfilling life.

We'll explore the art of breaking bad habits—the entrenched behaviors that hinder your progress and well-being. Armed with proven strategies, you'll learn how to identify triggers, confront cravings, and free yourself from the shackles of negative routines.

But it's not enough to break bad habits; you must also cultivate new, empowering ones. We'll dive deep into the science of habit formation, providing you with practical tools and techniques to build habits that align with your goals and aspirations.

Throughout this journey, we'll address common obstacles and setbacks that may arise. You'll discover strategies to maintain motivation, cope with relapses, and stay on course, even when faced with adversity.

Your Habit Reshaping Toolkit

This book is more than just theory; it's a practical guide to transforming your life through habits. You'll find exercises, case studies, and actionable steps in each chapter. These tools are designed to help you apply the principles of habit reshaping to your unique circumstances.

Additionally, real-life examples and success stories will illustrate how individuals from various backgrounds have reshaped their habits to achieve remarkable outcomes. These stories serve as inspiration and proof that you, too, can make lasting changes in your life.

A Call to Action

As we journey through the intricacies of habit reshaping, keep in mind that this is not a one-time read. It's a reference, a roadmap, and a companion on your path to personal growth and transformation.

Each chapter offers valuable insights and strategies that you can start applying immediately. The process of habit reshaping is ongoing, and with each step, you'll move closer to becoming the best version of yourself.

Are you ready to embark on this transformative journey? Are you ready to reshape your habits, unlock your potential, and design the life you desire? If your answer is yes, then let's begin. The power to reshape your habits—and your life—is in your hands.

1

Understanding Habits

The Habitual Mindset

Welcome to the fascinating world of habits. In this chapter, we will embark on a journey into the depths of habit formation, understanding what habits are, how they work, and why they are so crucial in our lives.

What Are Habits?

At their core, habits are a form of automated behavior. They are actions we perform with minimal conscious thought, often in response to specific cues or triggers. Think about your morning routine. You likely follow a sequence of actions almost automatically, from brushing your teeth to making coffee. These actions have become habits. Habits streamline our daily lives by reducing the mental effort required to make decisions.

Habitual Actions: Habits can encompass a wide range of behaviors, from the simple act of tying your shoelaces to more complex routines like preparing a meal or commuting to work. Whether they're mundane or sophisticated, habits are actions we perform routinely.

Automaticity: One key characteristic of habits is their automaticity. When a habit is formed, it becomes almost effortless to execute. You don't need to consciously think about each step; your brain executes the habit loop (cue, routine, reward) with minimal effort.

The Habit Loop

To truly understand habits, we must delve into the neurological processes that underlie them. The habit loop, a concept popularized by Charles Duhigg in his book "The Power of Habit," serves as the framework for understanding habit formation. It consists of three components:

1. Cue: This is the trigger that initiates a habit. It can be an external event, a specific time of day, an emotional state, or any other signal that prompts your brain to start a habitual action. For instance, feeling hungry (cue) might trigger the habit of snacking.

2. Routine: The routine is the actual behavior or action you perform in response to the cue. It's the habit itself. Using the previous example, the routine would be eating a snack when you feel hungry.

3. Reward: The reward is the positive outcome or satisfaction you gain from completing the routine. It reinforces the habit loop, making it more likely that you'll repeat the behavior in the future. In our example, the reward is the feeling of satisfaction and relief from hunger after snacking.

Understanding this loop is essential because it provides us with a roadmap for both building new habits and breaking bad ones. By manipulating the cue, routine, or reward, we can reshape our habits to align with our goals.

The Neuroscience of Habits

To comprehend the profound impact habits have on our lives, we must turn to the brain. Neuroscientists have made remarkable discoveries about the neural pathways involved in habit formation. One key region of interest is the basal ganglia.

The Basal Ganglia: This cluster of structures deep within the brain plays a central role in habit formation. It's responsible for encoding and storing habits based on the habit loop. When a behavior becomes habitual, it's the basal ganglia that takes over, allowing you to execute the routine without conscious effort.

The Prefrontal Cortex: In contrast to the basal ganglia, the prefrontal cortex is responsible for decision-making and conscious thought. When a behavior is novel or requires active decision-making, the prefrontal cortex is highly engaged. However, as a behavior becomes habitual, the prefrontal cortex's involvement diminishes.

This dynamic interaction between the basal ganglia and the prefrontal cortex explains why habits can be so challenging to change. Once a habit is deeply ingrained, it becomes a default response to a specific cue, and changing it requires effort and conscious intervention.

The Habitual Society

Habits aren't just confined to individuals; they shape entire societies and cultures. Consider the cultural habits around meal times in different countries. In Spain, it's customary to have a siesta (a midday nap) after lunch, while in Japan, it's common to bow as a sign of respect. These cultural norms are a product of ingrained habits passed down through generations.

Beyond cultural habits, societal systems and structures are influenced by collective behaviors. Traffic patterns, consumer habits, and even political ideologies reflect the habits of a society as a whole. The collective actions of millions of people shape the world we live in.

Habits and Systems: Think about the transportation systems in major cities. They are designed to accommodate the daily commuting habits of millions of people. From subways to bus routes, these systems are optimized based on the habitual behaviors of their users.

Cultural Norms: Cultural habits, such as greeting customs and social rituals, are deeply ingrained in societies. They dictate how people interact and relate to one another. Understanding these cultural habits is crucial for effective communication and integration.

Economic Impact: Consumer habits significantly influence economies. The buying patterns of individuals and households determine the success or failure of businesses. Companies spend vast sums of money studying consumer habits to tailor their products and marketing strategies.

The Habitual Life

Now that we've explored the fundamental aspects of habits, let's return to the individual level and consider the role of habits in our daily lives. Habits are, in many ways, the building blocks of our routines and behaviors.

Daily Routines: Your daily routines are composed of a series of habits. From waking up at a certain time to your morning hygiene rituals, your day is structured by these automatic behaviors.

Productivity: Habits play a crucial role in your work and productivity. Efficient work habits, such as task prioritization or time management, can significantly impact your professional success.

Health and Well-Being: Many aspects of health, including diet, exercise, and sleep, are governed by habits. Your eating habits, for example, can influence your weight, energy levels, and overall well-being.

Relationships: The way you interact with others is also influenced by habits. Communication habits, such as active listening or expressing gratitude, can strengthen your relationships.

Personal Growth: Finally, habits are key to personal growth and development. The pursuit of knowledge, self-improvement, and lifelong learning often relies on cultivating positive habits.

The Habitual Quest

As we navigate this chapter, it becomes evident that understanding and reshaping habits are not trivial endeavors. Habits are deeply ingrained in our lives, both as individuals and as members of society. But here's the exciting part: habits are malleable.

By gaining insights into how habits are formed and maintained, you gain the power to shape your own destiny. You can consciously cultivate good habits that propel you towards your goals while breaking free from the shackles of detrimental habits.

Throughout this book, we'll provide you with the tools, strategies, and real-world examples you need to embark on your habit reshaping journey. Whether you aim to become healthier, more productive, or more fulfilled, it all begins with understanding and reshaping your habits.

Key Takeaways

- Habits are automated behaviors that we perform with minimal conscious thought.

- The habit loop consists of a cue, routine, and reward, which is central to understanding habit formation.

- The basal ganglia and the prefrontal cortex are key brain regions involved in habit formation and conscious decision-making.

- Habits shape not only individuals but also societies and cultures.

- Habits influence daily routines, productivity, health, relationships, and personal growth.

2

Identifying Your Habits

The Habit of Self-Awareness

In the previous chapter, we delved deep into the science and psychology of habits, unraveling the intricacies of the habit loop and understanding how habits are formed and maintained. Armed with this knowledge, we are now prepared to take the next crucial step in our journey: identifying your habits.

The Habitual Blind Spot

Habits are so ingrained in our daily lives that they often go unnoticed. We perform them automatically, without conscious thought. As a result, we may be oblivious to the habits that shape our behaviors, both positive and negative.

This lack of awareness can be a significant barrier to personal growth and habit reshaping. How can you change something you're not even aware of? This chapter is dedicated to shining a light on your habits, making them visible, and understanding their impact.

Why Identify Your Habits?

Self-Discovery: Identifying your habits is an act of self-discovery. It allows you to gain a deeper understanding of who you are, how you operate, and why you make certain choices in your life.

Assessing Your Life: Your habits are the building blocks of your daily routines and behaviors. By examining your habits, you can assess various aspects of your life, from your health and productivity to your relationships and personal growth.

Creating a Baseline: Identifying your current habits provides a baseline from which you can measure your progress. It's the first step in determining which habits to keep, which to change, and which to discard.

Empowerment: Awareness of your habits gives you the power to make conscious choices. You can choose to reinforce positive habits, modify detrimental ones, and even develop new, empowering behaviors.

Goal Alignment: To achieve your goals and aspirations, it's essential to align your habits with your objectives. Identifying your habits is the first step in this alignment process.

Techniques for Habit Identification

Identifying your habits requires a mix of self-reflection, observation, and record-keeping. Here are several techniques to help you uncover your habits effectively:

1. Self-Reflection

Journaling: Keeping a journal is a powerful tool for self-reflection. Write down your daily routines, behaviors, and choices. Over time, patterns will emerge, revealing your habits.

Questioning: Ask yourself probing questions. What do you consistently do when you wake up? What habits do you have around meal times? How do you react when stressed? Questioning your actions can lead to habit discovery.

2. Observation

Third-Person Perspective: Imagine you're observing yourself from an outsider's point of view. This perspective shift can help you notice habits you might otherwise overlook.

Feedback from Others: Sometimes, those close to you can provide valuable insights into your habits. They may point out behaviors or routines that you've taken for granted.

3. Record-Keeping

Habit Tracking Apps: Numerous apps and tools are designed to help you track your habits. They provide a structured way to log your daily activities and visualize your habits over time.

Habit Scorecard: Create a habit scorecard by listing all your routines and behaviors. For each one, mark whether it's positive, negative, or neutral. This exercise can reveal patterns.

<u>Categories of Habits</u>

Habits can be categorized in various ways, depending on the aspect of your life you're examining. Here are some common categories of habits:

1. Personal Habits

- **Morning Routine:** Your habits upon waking up set the tone for the day. Do you reach for your phone, meditate, or exercise?

- **Hygiene:** Personal grooming habits, like brushing your teeth or showering, are often deeply ingrained.

- **Eating Habits:** Your dietary choices, portion sizes, and meal timing can all be habitual.

- **Sleep Routine:** The way you prepare for sleep and your bedtime rituals fall into this category.

2. Productivity and Work Habits

- **Task Prioritization:** How do you decide which tasks to tackle first? Do you follow a systematic approach?

- **Time Management:** Habits around time allocation, such as scheduling and sticking to deadlines, can greatly affect your productivity.

- **Workspace Organization:** The way you keep your workspace, whether cluttered or organized, can be habitual.

3. Health and Wellness Habits

- **Exercise Routine:** Whether you exercise regularly or not at all, your physical activity habits play a significant role in your health.

- **Dietary Habits:** Your eating patterns, food choices, and portion sizes all contribute to your overall health.

- **Stress Management:** How you cope with stress, whether through relaxation techniques or unhealthy habits like overeating, is essential for well-being.

4. Relationship Habits

- **Communication Habits:** The way you communicate with others, including active listening, empathy, or interrupting, falls into this category.

- **Conflict Resolution:** How you handle conflicts and disagreements with friends, family, or colleagues is influenced by your habits.

- **Expressing Gratitude:** Showing appreciation and gratitude to loved ones is a habit that strengthens relationships.

5. Personal Growth Habits

- **Learning Habits:** How you approach acquiring new knowledge, whether through reading, courses, or experiential learning, is a key personal growth habit.

- **Goal Setting:** Your habits around setting and pursuing goals can determine your level of achievement.

- **Self-Care:** Habits related to self-care, such as mindfulness, meditation, or journaling, are essential for personal growth.

Creating Your Habit Inventory

Now, let's take a practical step towards identifying your habits. Begin by creating a habit inventory—a list of your habits in various categories. You can use the following template as a starting point:

Category	Habit	Positive/ Negative/ Neutral	Notes
Personal Habits	Morning Routine		
	Hygiene		
	Eating Habits		
	Sleep Routine		
Productivity Habits	Task Prioritization		
	Time Management		
	Workspace Organization		
Health Habits	Exercise Routine		
	Dietary Habits		
	Stress Management		
Relationship Habits	Communication Habits		
	Conflict Resolution		
	Expressing Gratitude		
Personal Growth Habits	Learning Habits		
	Goal Setting		
	Self-Care		

This habit inventory is a living document. As you become more aware of your habits, you can continue to update and refine it.

Analyzing Your Habit Inventory

Once you've created your habit inventory, take some time to analyze it. Here are some questions to consider:

- Which habits do you consider positive and beneficial to your life?

- Are there any habits that you feel are holding you back or causing negative consequences?

- Do you notice patterns or themes in your habits? For example, do you have a tendency to procrastinate, or do you consistently prioritize self-care?

- Are there any surprises or insights that you've gained from this exercise?

Remember that this inventory is a tool for self-awareness, not judgment. It's an opportunity to better understand yourself and your behaviors.

The Power of Habit Tracking

While creating a habit inventory is a valuable first step, habit tracking can take your self-awareness to the next level. Habit tracking involves recording your habits on a daily or regular basis. It provides you with real-time data on your behavior and allows you to spot trends and changes over time.

Habit Tracking Apps: There are numerous habit-tracking apps available that make it easy to log your habits and view your progress. These apps often provide visual representations of your habits, making it easier to identify patterns.

Paper Journals: If you prefer a more analog approach, you can use a paper journal or habit-tracking template to record your habits daily. Some people find the act of physically writing down their habits to be more impactful.

Accountability Partners: Sharing your habit-tracking journey with a friend or accountability partner can provide motivation and support. You can hold each other accountable for sticking to your desired habits.

Habit Tracking Tips

Here are some tips to make habit tracking more effective:

- **Be Consistent:** Set a specific time each day to track your habits. Consistency is key to building a habit-tracking routine.

- **Start Small:** If tracking multiple habits feels overwhelming, start with just one or two. Once you've established the habit of tracking, you can gradually add more.

- **Use Reminders:** Set reminders or alarms on your phone to prompt you to track your habits at the designated time.

- **Be Honest:** Don't be tempted to embellish or omit information in your habit tracking. The goal is accurate self-assessment.

- **Celebrate Progress:** Acknowledge and celebrate your successes and progress along the way. Positive reinforcement can motivate you to maintain or improve your habits.

The Habitual Feedback Loop

As you identify and track your habits, you're essentially creating a feedback loop. This loop involves three essential steps:

1. Awareness: You become aware of your habits through self-reflection, observation, and tracking.

2. Analysis: You analyze your habits, identifying which ones align with your goals and which ones may need adjustment.

3. Action: Armed with this awareness and analysis, you take action. You may choose to reinforce positive habits, modify detrimental ones, or develop new behaviors.

This feedback loop is at the heart of habit reshaping. It empowers you to make informed decisions about which habits to keep, change, or discard.

Case Study: Sarah's Habitual Discovery

To illustrate the power of habit identification, let's consider the story of Sarah, a young professional looking to improve her work-life balance and well-being.

Sarah's Challenge: Sarah felt overwhelmed by her hectic work schedule and found herself often working late into the evening. She wanted to reclaim her evenings for relaxation and self-care.

Habit Identification: Through self-reflection and habit tracking, Sarah identified several work-related habits that contributed to her long work hours:

- **Habit:** Checking work emails after dinner.

- Habit: Taking on additional tasks even when her workload was already substantial.

- Habit: Allowing work-related stress to spill over into her personal time.

Analysis: Sarah recognized that these habits were contributing to her work-life imbalance and causing her stress and fatigue.

Action: Sarah decided to take action. She set boundaries for checking work emails, learned to say no to additional tasks when her plate was full, and implemented relaxation techniques to manage work-related stress. Over time, these changes allowed her to reclaim her evenings and improve her well-being.

Sarah's story exemplifies the transformative power of habit identification. By becoming aware of her habits and taking purposeful action, she was able to reshape her routines to align with her well-being goals.

Key Takeaways

- Identifying your habits is a critical step toward personal growth and habit reshaping.

- Techniques for habit identification include self-reflection, observation, and record-keeping.

- Habits can be categorized into various areas of your life, such as personal, productivity, health, relationships, and personal growth.

- Creating a habit inventory and tracking your habits provide valuable insights into your behavior.

- The habit feedback loop involves awareness, analysis, and action and is essential for reshaping habits.

3

The Power of Good Habits

Introduction: The Habitual Path to Transformation

In the previous chapters, we embarked on a journey into the world of habits. We explored the science behind habit formation, learned how to identify our habits, and understood why habits are so crucial in our lives. Now, we dive deeper into the heart of habit reshaping by focusing on the transformative power of good habits.

Good habits are the key to unlocking your full potential and achieving your goals. Whether you aspire to become healthier, more productive, or more fulfilled, the path begins with cultivating positive routines. In this chapter, we'll explore the profound impact of good habits and uncover strategies to build and sustain them.

The Benefits of Good Habits

Why are good habits so essential for personal growth and well-being? Let's begin by exploring the numerous benefits that come with cultivating positive routines.

1. Consistency

Good habits provide a framework for consistency in your life. When you have established routines, you're more likely to stick to your goals and stay on track. Consistency is the cornerstone of progress.

2. Efficiency

Positive habits streamline your daily activities, making you more efficient. You waste less time on decision-making and deliberation because your habits dictate your actions. This efficiency frees up time and mental energy for other pursuits.

3. Progress

Good habits are catalysts for progress. They enable you to take incremental steps toward your goals, ensuring that you make steady progress over time. Progress, no matter how small, is a powerful motivator.

4. Discipline

Cultivating positive routines requires discipline. This discipline spills over into other areas of your life, enhancing your self-control and willpower. It's a skill that can be honed through habit formation.

5. Well-Being

Many good habits are directly related to well-being. Habits such as regular exercise, a balanced diet, and sufficient sleep contribute to physical and mental health. They enhance your overall quality of life.

6. Personal Growth

Good habits are a vehicle for personal growth. They enable you to acquire new skills, gain knowledge, and expand your horizons. Whether it's reading daily, learning a new language, or practicing a musical instrument, habits foster growth.

7. Goal Achievement

Achieving your goals often depends on the consistent pursuit of specific actions. Good habits align with your goals and provide the roadmap for their attainment. They turn aspirations into concrete steps.

The Science of Good Habits

What distinguishes good habits from bad ones? While the habit loop (cue, routine, reward) remains the same, the difference lies in the nature of the routine and its outcomes.

Positive Feedback Loop: Good habits are characterized by a positive feedback loop. When you engage in a positive routine, you receive a rewarding experience that reinforces the habit. For example, after exercising (routine), you feel energized and accomplished (reward), which reinforces the habit of exercising.

Neurological Changes: Engaging in good habits triggers neurological changes in your brain. Over time, these changes strengthen the neural pathways associated with the habit, making it more automatic and effortless.

Increased Dopamine: Positive habits are often associated with the release of dopamine, a neurotransmitter linked to pleasure and reward. This dopamine release creates a sense of satisfaction and reinforces the habit loop.

The Compound Effect

One of the most remarkable aspects of good habits is their compounding effect. The idea is simple: small, consistent actions, when repeated over time, lead to significant results. This concept is beautifully illustrated by the story of the "doubling penny."

Imagine you have a magic penny that doubles in value every day. On the first day, it's worth one cent. On the second day, it doubles to two cents, then four cents, eight cents, and so on. After 30 days, that seemingly insignificant penny would have grown to over $5 million.

This analogy illustrates the power of consistent, incremental growth. Good habits work in a similar way. Each day you engage in a positive routine, you're making a small investment in your future. Over time, these investments accumulate, leading to remarkable transformations in your life.

The Keystone Habit

Some habits are like keystones in an arch. They have a disproportionately positive impact on various aspects of your life. These are known as keystone habits. When you cultivate a keystone habit, it often triggers a ripple effect, influencing other habits and behaviors.

Example: Regular exercise is often considered a keystone habit. When you commit to regular workouts, it tends to lead to improvements in diet, sleep quality, stress management, and even productivity. Exercise serves as the keystone that supports other positive changes.

Identifying Keystone Habits: Keystone habits are unique to each person, but they typically have a few common characteristics:

- They have a ripple effect, positively influencing multiple areas of your life.

- They often lead to the development of other good habits.

- They serve as a catalyst for personal growth and well-being.

Cultivating Good Habits

Now that we understand the power and benefits of good habits, let's explore strategies to cultivate them effectively. Building positive routines is not a matter of luck; it's a systematic process that anyone can undertake.

1. Start Small

The Power of Tiny Habits: Begin with small, manageable habits. This approach, popularized by behavior scientist BJ Fogg, is based on the idea that tiny habits are easy to adopt and can serve as building blocks for larger changes. For example, instead of aiming to run a marathon, start with the habit of walking for 10 minutes each day.

The Two-Minute Rule: If a habit seems daunting, break it down into a two-minute version. The idea is to make the habit so easy that you can't say no. For instance, if you want to read more, start with the habit of reading for just two minutes a day. Once you've established the habit, you can gradually increase the duration.

2. Set SMART Goals

Specific: Define your habit in clear, specific terms. Instead of a vague goal like "get fit," specify "exercise for 30 minutes every morning."

Measurable: Establish criteria to measure your progress. Use metrics like time, frequency, or quantity to track your habit. For example, "drink eight glasses of water daily" is measurable.

Achievable: Ensure that your habit is realistic and attainable. Setting an unattainable goal can lead to frustration and demotivation.

Relevant: Your habit should align with your goals and values. It should have a purpose and meaning in your life.

Time-Bound: Set a specific timeframe for your habit. For instance, "practice mindfulness meditation for 10 minutes every evening before bed."

3. Create a Habit Loop

Remember the habit loop—cue, routine, reward. Design your habit loop intentionally:

- **Cue:** Identify a cue or trigger that prompts your habit. This could be a specific time of day, an existing routine, or an environmental cue.

- **Routine:** Define the action you'll take as part of your habit. Be clear about what you need to do.

- **Reward:** Consider the reward you'll receive after completing your habit. Make it something satisfying and motivating.

4. Track Your Progress

Habit tracking is a powerful tool for accountability and motivation. Whether you use a habit-tracking app, journal, or a simple calendar, regularly record your habit-related activities. Tracking provides a visual representation of your progress and reinforces your commitment.

5. Stay Consistent

Consistency is key to habit formation. Aim to perform your habit at the same time and in the same context each day. Consistency helps solidify the habit and make it a natural part of your routine.

6. Use Positive Reinforcement

Reward yourself for sticking to your habit. Positive reinforcement enhances the habit loop by associating the routine with a pleasurable experience. Treat yourself to something you enjoy after completing your habit, whether it's a small treat, a few moments of relaxation, or a sense of accomplishment.

7. Leverage Social Accountability

Share your habit goals with a friend, family member, or accountability partner. Knowing that someone else is aware of your commitment can boost your motivation and provide a sense of external accountability.

8. Overcome Setbacks

Expect setbacks and slip-ups along the way. Habits take time to establish, and occasional failures are part of the process. The key is to learn from setbacks, adjust your approach if needed, and continue moving forward.

Case Study: Alex's Habit Transformation

To illustrate the transformative power of good habits, let's explore the story of Alex, a young professional seeking to enhance his productivity and work-life balance.

Alex's Challenge: Alex often felt overwhelmed by his demanding job and struggled to find time for his personal projects and hobbies.

Habit Transformation: Alex identified time management as a keystone habit that could improve his life in multiple ways. He started by implementing the following habits:

- **Morning Routine:** Alex established a morning routine that included meditation, exercise, and a healthy breakfast. This routine helped him start his day with clarity and energy.

- **Task Prioritization:** He developed a habit of prioritizing his tasks and creating a to-do list for the day. This practice allowed him to focus on high-impact activities.

- **Time Blocking:** Alex adopted the habit of time blocking, scheduling dedicated periods for focused work, meetings, and breaks. This habit enhanced his productivity and time management skills.

Transformation: Over time, these habits had a profound impact on Alex's life. He became more productive at work, allowing him to leave the office on time. This newfound free time enabled him to pursue his personal interests and hobbies, leading to a greater sense of fulfillment and work-life balance.

Alex's story illustrates how cultivating good habits, even in one area of life, can trigger a positive ripple effect that enhances various aspects of well-being.

<u>**Key Takeaways**</u>

- Good habits offer numerous benefits, including consistency, efficiency, progress, discipline, well-being, personal growth, and goal achievement.

- The science of good habits involves positive feedback loops, neurological changes, and the release of dopamine.

- Keystone habits have a disproportionate positive impact on multiple areas of life.

- Strategies for cultivating good habits include starting small, setting SMART goals, creating a habit loop, tracking progress, staying consistent, using positive reinforcement, leveraging social accountability, and overcoming setbacks.

4

Breaking Bad Habits

Introduction: The Art of Transformation

Breaking bad habits is a crucial step on the path to personal growth and success. In this chapter, we'll explore the psychology of habit formation and the strategies that empower you to overcome undesirable behaviors. Whether you're looking to break habits related to procrastination, unhealthy eating, smoking, or any other detrimental pattern, the insights and techniques discussed here will guide you toward lasting change and a more fulfilling life.

The Nature of Habits

Habits are deeply ingrained routines that influence our daily lives, often on autopilot. While good habits can propel us forward, bad habits can hold us back.

The Habit Loop

Habits typically follow a loop that consists of three stages:

1. Cue/Trigger: The habit begins with a cue or trigger, which is a signal that initiates the behavior. This can be a specific time of day, an emotional state, or a particular location.

2. Routine/Behavior: The routine is the habitual behavior itself, such as smoking a cigarette, snacking when stressed, or procrastinating on work.

3. Reward: Habits persist because they offer some form of reward or satisfaction. The reward reinforces the habit loop.

Habit Formation

Habits are formed through repetition. When a behavior is consistently followed by a rewarding outcome, the brain associates the cue with the routine, making the habit more automatic.

Understanding Bad Habits

To break bad habits effectively, it's crucial to understand their underlying causes and triggers.

Common Bad Habits

Procrastination: Delaying tasks or avoiding responsibilities, leading to stress and decreased productivity.

Unhealthy Eating: Consuming excessive junk food, sugar, or unhealthy snacks, which can impact physical health.

Smoking: The addictive habit of smoking cigarettes, which poses significant health risks.

Nail Biting: A common nervous habit that can harm nails and dental health.

Excessive Screen Time: Spending excessive hours on screens, including smartphones, computers, and TV, which can lead to various negative consequences.

Habit Triggers

Stress: Many bad habits are triggered by stress or negative emotions as individuals seek relief or distraction.

Boredom: A lack of stimulating activities or interests can lead to habits like mindless snacking or excessive screen time.

Peer Pressure: Social situations and peer influence can reinforce bad habits, such as smoking or excessive drinking.

Environment: Specific locations or contexts can trigger habits. For example, entering a fast-food restaurant might trigger unhealthy eating habits.

Strategies for Breaking Bad Habits

Breaking bad habits requires a deliberate and systematic approach. Here are effective strategies to help you overcome undesirable behaviors.

Self-Awareness

Identify Triggers: Recognize the cues or triggers that prompt your bad habits. Keep a journal to track when and why these habits occur.

Understand the Reward: Analyze the reward you get from the habit. Understanding the underlying satisfaction can help you find healthier alternatives.

Mindfulness: Practice mindfulness to increase awareness of your actions and reactions. This can help you pause before engaging in a bad habit.

Replacement Habits

Identify Healthy Alternatives: Find alternative behaviors that satisfy the same needs as the bad habit. For example, if stress triggers snacking, try deep breathing or a short walk instead.

Positive Reinforcement: Reward yourself when you successfully replace a bad habit with a healthy one. This reinforces the new behavior.

Start Small: Begin with manageable changes. Gradual progress is often more sustainable than attempting a complete overhaul.

Gradual Reduction

Set Limits: If quitting cold turkey seems daunting, set clear limits on the bad habit. For example, reduce the number of cigarettes smoked per day or allocate a specific time for screen use.

Incremental Reduction: Gradually decrease the frequency or intensity of the habit over time.

Track Progress: Keep a record of your gradual reduction efforts to monitor your success and adjust your approach as needed.

Social Support

Accountability Partner: Share your goal of breaking the bad habit with a trusted friend or family member who can provide support and encouragement.

Support Groups: Join a support group or community of individuals who are also working to break similar habits.

Professional Help: Consider seeking professional help, such as therapy or counseling, for habit-breaking assistance.

Habit Disruption

Change the Environment: Modify your environment to reduce exposure to triggers. For example, remove unhealthy snacks from your pantry.

Visual Cues: Create visual reminders of your commitment to breaking the habit, such as notes or images on your phone or computer.

Delay Gratification: When the urge for the bad habit arises, delay gratification by waiting for a set period before acting on it. The craving often subsides.

Case Study: Mark's Journey to Quit Smoking

To illustrate the process of breaking a bad habit, let's explore Mark's story. Mark had been a smoker for over a decade and wanted to quit to improve his health and save money.

Mark's Challenge: Mark faced the challenge of nicotine addiction and the habitual nature of smoking.

Habit-Breaking Transformation: Recognizing the need for change, Mark embarked on a journey to quit smoking by implementing several strategies:

- Self-Awareness: Mark tracked his smoking triggers and identified stress as a significant cue.

- **Replacement Habits:** He replaced smoking with chewing gum and deep breathing exercises when stress hit.

- **Gradual Reduction:** Mark gradually reduced the number of cigarettes he smoked each day.

- **Social Support:** He shared his goal with his wife, who offered emotional support and encouragement.

- **Professional Help:** Mark sought the assistance of a smoking cessation program and attended counseling sessions.

Transformation: Over time, these habit-breaking strategies allowed Mark to quit smoking successfully. His journey highlights that breaking a bad habit often requires a combination of self-awareness, support, and structured approaches.

Key Takeaways

- Habits follow a loop consisting of cues/triggers, routines/behaviors, and rewards.

- Understanding the triggers and rewards of bad habits is essential for breaking them.

- Effective strategies for breaking bad habits include self-awareness, replacement habits, gradual reduction, social support, and habit disruption.

- Breaking a bad habit often requires persistence and a multifaceted approach.

5

Building Good Habits

Introduction: The Power of Positive Change

Building good habits is the key to personal growth, success, and lasting transformation. In this chapter, we'll explore the science behind habit formation and the strategies that empower you to cultivate positive behaviors. Whether you're aiming to establish habits related to productivity, fitness, mindfulness, or any other area of your life, the insights and techniques discussed here will guide you toward positive change and a more fulfilling future.

The Science of Habit Formation

Habits are not simply a matter of willpower; they are deeply ingrained in our brains. Understanding the science behind habit formation can help you build and sustain good habits more effectively.

The Habit Loop Revisited

As mentioned earlier, habits follow a loop with three key components:

1. Cue/Trigger: The habit starts with a cue or trigger, which prompts the behavior.

2. Routine/Behavior: This is the actual habit or behavior you want to establish.

3. Reward: The reward is the positive outcome or satisfaction you gain from the behavior.

The Habit Loop in the Brain

Neuroscientists have discovered that habits are etched into our brains through a process involving the basal ganglia, a region responsible for motor functions and learning. Here's how it works:

- **Cue:** The cue signals the brain to initiate the habit, creating a craving.

- **Routine:** You perform the habit or behavior in response to the craving.

- **Reward:** The brain associates the routine with a reward, reinforcing the habit loop.

Neuroplasticity and Habit Formation

The brain's ability to change and adapt, known as neuroplasticity, plays a pivotal role in habit formation. When you consistently perform a behavior and experience a reward, your brain rewires itself to make that behavior more automatic.

The Anatomy of Good Habits

Good habits have the power to transform your life positively. Whether it's adopting a healthy lifestyle, becoming more organized, or enhancing your skills, the process of building good habits remains consistent.

Defining Good Habits

Alignment with Goals: Good habits align with your long-term goals and values, bringing you closer to the life you envision.

Sustainable: Good habits are sustainable over time, allowing you to maintain them as part of your daily routine.

Incremental Progress: They promote incremental progress, helping you make consistent strides toward your objectives.

Common Good Habits

Exercise Routine: Establishing a regular exercise routine contributes to physical health and well-being.

Healthy Eating: Cultivating healthy eating habits supports your overall health and vitality.

Productivity and Time Management: Developing habits related to productivity and time management enhances efficiency and goal achievement.

Mindfulness and Meditation: Incorporating mindfulness and meditation practices fosters mental clarity, emotional balance, and stress reduction.

Lifelong Learning: Building a habit of continuous learning and skill development promotes personal and professional growth.

Strategies for Building Good Habits

Building good habits requires a deliberate and systematic approach. Here are effective strategies to help you cultivate positive behaviors.

Start Small

Tiny Habits: Begin with "tiny habits" that are so small they feel effortless. These can serve as a gateway to larger changes.

Behavior Anchors: Attach your new habit to an existing habit or routine. For example, if you want to establish a reading habit, do it right after your morning coffee.

Consistency Over Intensity: Prioritize consistency over intensity. Aim to perform the habit regularly, even if it's in small increments.

Clear and Specific Goals

Define Your Habit: Clearly define the habit you want to build. Be specific about what it entails.

SMART Goals: Apply the SMART (Specific, Measurable, Achievable, Relevant, Time-bound) framework to your habit goals.

Visualize Success: Visualize yourself successfully completing the habit to reinforce your commitment.

Habit Stacking

Create Chains: Link multiple habits together into a "habit chain." Completing one habit triggers the next.

Utilize Triggers: Use natural triggers or cues in your environment to prompt your habit. For example, the sound of your morning alarm can signal the start of your exercise routine.

Track Progress: Maintain a habit tracker to monitor your consistency and progress.

Accountability and Support

Public Commitment: Share your habit-building goal publicly to create a sense of accountability.

Accountability Partner: Partner with a friend or family member who has a similar habit-building goal. Check in with each other regularly.

Join a Community: Join an online or local community focused on the habit you're trying to build. Engaging with like-minded individuals can provide motivation and support.

Rewards and Positive Reinforcement

Immediate Rewards: Create immediate rewards for yourself after completing the habit. These can be small treats or moments of relaxation.

Celebrate Milestones: Celebrate your achievements and milestones along the way. Acknowledging your progress boosts motivation.

Track Benefits: Keep a record of the positive changes and benefits you experience as a result of your habit.

Self-Compassion and Patience

Be Kind to Yourself: Embrace self-compassion and avoid self-criticism when you face setbacks or miss a day. Habits take time to solidify.

Resilience: Develop resilience by recognizing that occasional slips or failures are part of the habit-building process.

Adjust and Iterate: If a particular approach isn't working, be open to adjusting your strategy. Habits can be tailored to suit your unique circumstances and preferences.

<u>Case Study: Lisa's Journey to a Morning Routine</u>

To illustrate the process of building a good habit, let's explore Lisa's story. Lisa wanted to establish a morning routine that would set a positive tone for her day.

Lisa's Challenge: Lisa faced the challenge of feeling rushed and disorganized in the mornings, leading to stress.

Habit-Building Transformation: Recognizing the need for change, Lisa embarked on a journey to build a morning routine by implementing several strategies:

- **Starting Small:** She began with a tiny habit of taking a few moments for deep breathing upon waking.

- **Clear Goals:** Lisa defined her morning routine, including activities like meditation, stretching, and planning her day.

- **Habit Stacking:** She anchored her new routine to her existing habit of making coffee each morning.

- **Positive Reinforcement:** Lisa rewarded herself with a cup of her favorite tea after completing her morning routine.

- **Resilience:** When she missed a day, Lisa forgave herself and continued with her habit the next morning.

Transformation: Over time, these habit-building strategies allowed Lisa to establish a morning routine that reduced stress and increased her sense of control over her day. Her journey highlights the importance of patience and self-compassion when building good habits.

<u>**Key Takeaways**</u>

- Building good habits is essential for personal growth, success, and lasting transformation.

- Habits follow a consistent loop involving cues/triggers, routines/behaviors, and rewards.

- Effective strategies for building good habits include starting small, setting clear goals, habit stacking, seeking accountability and support, utilizing rewards and positive reinforcement, and practicing self-compassion and patience.

- Consistency and gradual progress are key to habit-building success.

6

Personal Growth and Development Habits

Introduction: The Journey Within

Personal growth and development are lifelong journeys that lead to self-discovery, self-improvement, and a deeper sense of fulfillment. In this chapter, we'll explore the habits that promote personal growth, self-awareness, and continuous learning. Whether you're striving to unlock your full potential, expand your horizons, or overcome obstacles, the habits discussed here will empower you to embark on a transformative journey.

The Significance of Personal Growth

Personal growth is not just a pursuit; it's a way of life. It encompasses self-improvement, self-awareness, and the quest to become the best version of yourself.

Why Personal Growth Matters

Self-Discovery: Personal growth encourages self-exploration and self-discovery, helping you better understand your values, strengths, and weaknesses.

Self-Improvement: It empowers you to identify areas for improvement and develop the skills and qualities you aspire to possess.

Adaptability: Personal growth equips you with the resilience and adaptability needed to navigate life's challenges and changes.

Fulfillment: The pursuit of personal growth often leads to increased life satisfaction, happiness, and a sense of purpose.

Impact on Others: Your personal growth journey can inspire and positively influence those around you, fostering a culture of continuous improvement.

Habits for Personal Growth and Development

Personal growth and development are nurtured by intentional habits that encourage self-reflection, learning, and self-improvement.

Self-Reflection

Journaling: Maintain a journal to record your thoughts, feelings, and experiences. Regular journaling promotes self-awareness and emotional clarity.

Meditation: Incorporate meditation into your routine to cultivate mindfulness, self-observation, and inner peace.

Self-Review: Periodically assess your progress, goals, and areas for improvement. Set aside dedicated time for self-review.

Goal Setting

Long-Term Goals: Define long-term goals that align with your values and aspirations. These goals serve as a compass for your personal growth journey.

Short-Term Goals: Break long-term goals into smaller, achievable milestones. Short-term goals provide a sense of progress and motivation.

SMART Goals: Employ the SMART (Specific, Measurable, Achievable, Relevant, Time-bound) criteria to set clear and actionable goals.

Continuous Learning

Reading Habit: Cultivate a habit of reading regularly. Explore books, articles, and resources that broaden your knowledge and perspective.

Online Courses: Take advantage of online courses and platforms to acquire new skills or deepen your understanding of subjects of interest.

Skill Development: Identify skills you'd like to acquire or improve and invest time in developing them.

Embracing Challenges

Embrace Failure: View failure as a stepping stone to growth rather than a setback. Learn from your mistakes and use them as opportunities for improvement.

Step Outside Your Comfort Zone: Challenge yourself to try new experiences, face fears, and embrace discomfort. Growth often occurs outside your comfort zone.

Resilience: Cultivate resilience by adopting a growth mindset. Believe in your ability to learn and adapt in the face of adversity.

Self-Care Habits

Self-care is a fundamental component of personal growth and well-being. It involves practices that nourish your physical, emotional, and mental health.

Physical Self-Care

Exercise Routine: Engage in regular physical activity that promotes fitness and overall health.

Nutrition: Maintain a balanced and nutritious diet that provides essential nutrients for your body.

Adequate Sleep: Prioritize sleep and establish good sleep hygiene practices for optimal rest.

Emotional Self-Care

Emotional Expression: Express your feelings and emotions through outlets like journaling, art, or talking with a trusted friend.

Mindfulness: Practice mindfulness techniques, such as meditation and deep breathing, to stay grounded in the present moment.

Stress Management: Develop effective stress management strategies to cope with life's challenges.

Mental Self-Care

Learning and Intellectual Stimulation: Engage in activities that stimulate your mind, such as reading, puzzles, or learning new skills.

Positive Affirmations: Use positive affirmations to boost self-esteem and maintain a positive mindset.

Mental Health Support: Seek professional help or therapy if you're facing mental health challenges. Reaching out for support is a sign of strength.

Time Management for Personal Growth

Effective time management habits help you allocate your time to personal growth activities, ensuring you make consistent progress.

Prioritization

Prioritize Personal Growth: Allocate dedicated time each day or week for personal growth activities, such as reading or skill development.

Eliminate Time-Wasting Habits: Identify and reduce activities that consume your time without contributing to your growth or well-being.

Time Blocking: Schedule specific time blocks for personal growth tasks and protect these appointments as you would any other commitment.

Focus and Productivity

Minimize Distractions: Create a distraction-free environment when working on personal growth tasks.

Use Productivity Techniques: Incorporate productivity techniques like the Pomodoro Technique to maximize focus and efficiency.

Set Clear Goals: Clearly define what you want to achieve during your personal growth time to maintain purpose and motivation.

Personal Growth Accountability

Accountability is a powerful motivator for personal growth. Establishing accountability habits ensures you stay committed to your journey.

Accountability Partners

Find a Mentor: Seek a mentor or coach who can provide guidance, support, and accountability in your personal growth efforts.

Accountability Groups: Join or create an accountability group with friends or peers who share similar growth goals.

Regular Check-Ins: Set up regular check-in meetings with your accountability partner or group to review progress and set new goals.

Tracking Progress

Goal Tracking: Monitor your progress toward your personal growth goals using a journal, app, or checklist.

Celebrate Milestones: Celebrate your achievements and milestones along your personal growth journey. Acknowledging progress boosts motivation.

Course Correction: Be open to adjusting your goals or strategies if you encounter challenges or changes in your aspirations.

Case Study: Alex's Journey to Personal Growth

To illustrate the power of personal growth and development habits, let's explore Alex's story. Alex, a young professional, felt stuck In a career that no longer fulfilled him.

Alex's Challenge: Alex struggled with a sense of purpose and wanted to explore new career opportunities.

Personal Growth Transformation: Recognizing the need for change, Alex embarked on a personal growth journey by adopting various habits:

- **Self-Reflection:** Alex began journaling to explore his passions and values.

- **Goal Setting:** He set clear, SMART goals for his career transition and personal development.

- **Continuous Learning:** Alex took online courses and attended workshops to acquire new skills.

- **Networking:** He expanded his professional network, seeking mentors and like-minded individuals.

Transformation: Over time, these personal growth and development habits led Alex to make a career change, aligning his work with his passions and values. His journey demonstrates that intentional habits can lead to significant personal transformation and fulfillment.

Key Takeaways

- Personal growth and development are lifelong journeys that lead to self-improvement, self-awareness, and fulfillment.

- Habits for personal growth include self-reflection, goal setting, continuous learning, and embracing challenges.

- Self-care habits nourish physical, emotional, and mental well-being, supporting personal growth.

- Effective time management ensures you allocate time to personal growth activities.

- Accountability habits, such as finding mentors or tracking progress, help
maintain commitment to personal growth goals.

7
Productivity and Success Habits

Introduction: The Path to Achievement

Success is often the result of consistent effort and intentional habits. In this chapter, we'll explore the habits that boost productivity, enhance time management, and lay the foundation for success in various aspects of your life. Whether you're striving for professional accomplishments or personal goals, the habits we'll discuss can propel you forward on your journey to success.

The Power of Productivity

Productivity is the art of efficiently and effectively using your time and resources to achieve your goals. It's not about working harder but working smarter. Productive habits are essential because they enable you to maximize your output while minimizing wasted time and effort.

Why Productivity Matters

Goal Achievement: Productivity habits help you make progress toward your goals. Whether it's completing a project, advancing in your career, or pursuing personal ambitions, productivity is the engine that drives achievement.

Time Management: Productivity habits improve time management skills, allowing you to allocate your time wisely. This means spending more time on meaningful tasks and less on distractions or low-priority activities.

Reduced Stress: When you're productive, you can meet deadlines, fulfill commitments, and prevent last-minute rushes. This reduces stress and increases your sense of control.

Quality Work: Productivity isn't just about quantity; it's also about the quality of your work. By focusing on productivity, you can produce high-quality results efficiently.

Work-Life Balance: Effective productivity habits can free up more time for personal life, hobbies, and relaxation, promoting a healthy work-life balance.

Time Management Habits

Time management is the foundation of productivity. Effective time management habits enable you to make the most of your day, reduce procrastination, and accomplish tasks efficiently.

Prioritization

Eisenhower Matrix: Prioritize tasks using the Eisenhower Matrix, which categorizes tasks into four quadrants based on urgency and importance:

- **Urgent and Important:** Do these tasks immediately.

- **Important but Not Urgent:** Schedule these tasks for later.

- **Urgent but Not Important:** Delegate these tasks if possible.

- **Neither Urgent nor Important:** Consider eliminating or minimizing these tasks.

To-Do Lists: Create daily or weekly to-do lists, highlighting the most important and time-sensitive items.

Time Blocking: Allocate specific blocks of time for different tasks or activities. This helps you maintain focus and avoid multitasking.

Organization

Digital Tools: Utilize digital tools and apps for task management, scheduling, and reminders.

Calendar: Maintain a well-organized calendar to track appointments, deadlines, and events.

Declutter: Keep your physical and digital workspace organized and clutter-free.

Goal Setting

SMART Goals: Set Specific, Measurable, Achievable, Relevant, and Time-bound goals. SMART goals provide clear direction and motivation.

Big-Picture Planning: Align your daily tasks with your long-term goals. This ensures that your actions contribute to your broader objectives.

Time Management Techniques

Pomodoro Technique: Work in focused, 25-minute intervals (Pomodoros) with short breaks in between. This method helps maintain concentration and productivity.

Two-Minute Rule: If a task takes less than two minutes to complete, do it immediately rather than postponing it.

Batching: Group similar tasks together and tackle them during dedicated time blocks. For example, respond to emails or make phone calls during designated periods.

Focus and Concentration Habits

In our modern, fast-paced world, maintaining focus and concentration is increasingly challenging. However, cultivating habits that enhance focus can significantly boost productivity.

Mindfulness

Meditation: Regular mindfulness meditation improves attention, reduces stress, and enhances cognitive function.

Deep Work: Embrace the concept of "deep work" by dedicating uninterrupted, focused time to challenging tasks.

Limit Distractions: Identify and minimize distractions in your environment, whether they are digital notifications, clutter, or noise.

Prioritization and Single-Tasking

Priority-Based Work: Identify your most important task for the day and tackle it first. This minimizes decision fatigue and ensures you invest your best energy where it matters most.

Single-Tasking: Avoid multitasking, as it can reduce efficiency and quality of work. Instead, focus on one task at a time.

Time Management Tools

Time Tracking: Use time tracking apps or methods to monitor how you spend your time. This awareness can help you identify areas for improvement.

Digital Detox: Occasionally disconnect from digital devices and platforms to regain focus and mental clarity.

Proactive Habits

Proactive habits involve taking initiative, planning ahead, and staying ahead of potential issues. These habits are essential for success, as they help you anticipate challenges and seize opportunities.

Planning and Goal Setting

Weekly Planning: Set aside time each week to review your goals, plan tasks, and assess your progress.

Anticipate Challenges: Identify potential obstacles and develop contingency plans to address them.

Adaptability: Be open to adjusting your plans as needed. Flexibility allows you to navigate unexpected changes effectively.

Learning and Growth

Continuous Learning: Cultivate a habit of lifelong learning by regularly acquiring new knowledge and skills relevant to your goals.

Feedback: Seek feedback from peers, mentors, or colleagues to identify areas for improvement.

Self-Reflection: Dedicate time for self-reflection to assess your strengths, weaknesses, and areas for personal growth.

Networking and Relationship Building

Networking: Develop a habit of expanding your professional network. Attend industry events, connect with peers, and nurture valuable relationships.

Relationship Building: Strengthen existing relationships by showing appreciation and support. Building positive connections can lead to opportunities and collaborations.

Time-Saving Habits

Time-saving habits involve streamlining processes, automating tasks, and reducing unnecessary activities. These habits free up more time for meaningful pursuits.

Automation

Task Automation: Identify repetitive tasks that can be automated using software or tools. This reduces manual effort and saves time.

Email Filters: Use email filters and rules to organize and prioritize your inbox. This minimizes the time spent sorting through emails.

Delegation

Delegation: Delegate tasks to capable team members or assistants when appropriate. Effective delegation frees you to focus on high-impact activities.

Outsourcing: Consider outsourcing tasks or projects that fall outside your expertise or are time-consuming.

Minimalism

Minimalism: Embrace minimalism in both your physical and digital life. Reduce clutter, unnecessary possessions, and distractions.

Digital Minimalism: Simplify your digital life by minimizing the number of apps, notifications, and subscriptions.

Case Study: James's Journey to Success

To illustrate the power of productivity and success habits, let's explore James's story. James, a young entrepreneur, was determined to grow his startup but often felt overwhelmed by his workload.

James's Challenge: James struggled with time management and often found himself working long hours without achieving his desired results.

Productivity and Success Transformation: James recognized the need for change and began cultivating productivity and success habits:

- **Goal-Oriented Planning:** He adopted SMART goal setting and weekly planning to prioritize tasks that aligned with his startup's growth.

- **Focus on Deep Work:** James implemented deep work sessions, eliminating distractions during specific time blocks to tackle critical tasks.

- Delegation: Recognizing that he couldn't do everything himself, James learned to delegate non-core tasks to his team.

- Continuous Learning: He committed to ongoing learning, attending workshops and reading books on entrepreneurship and leadership.

Transformation: Over time, these productivity and success habits had a remarkable impact on James's entrepreneurial journey. He achieved significant milestones, expanded his startup, and achieved his goals. His story illustrates how intentional habits can drive success and fulfillment.

<u>Key Takeaways</u>

- Productivity habits enable you to achieve goals efficiently and reduce stress.

- Time management habits are essential for effective task allocation and goal prioritization.

- Focus and concentration habits enhance productivity by minimizing distractions.

- Proactive habits involve planning, adaptability, continuous learning, and relationship building.

- Time-saving habits streamline processes, automate tasks, and minimize unnecessary activities.

8

Health and Wellness Habits

Introduction: The Foundation of Well-Being

Your health is your most valuable asset. It's the foundation upon which you build your life, pursue your goals, and find fulfillment. In this chapter, we'll explore the essential role of health and wellness habits in shaping your physical and mental well-being. From exercise and nutrition to stress management and sleep, we'll delve into the habits that promote vitality and a balanced life.

The Mind-Body Connection

Before we dive into specific health and wellness habits, it's essential to acknowledge the profound connection between your mind and body. Your mental and emotional well-being significantly impact your physical health, and vice versa. This mind-body connection underscores the importance of holistic self-care.

Stress and Health

Stress is a natural part of life, but chronic stress can have detrimental effects on your health. It can lead to high blood pressure, weakened immune function, and increased risk of chronic diseases. Stress management, therefore, is a crucial component of overall well-being.

Mindfulness Practices: Techniques like meditation, deep breathing exercises, and yoga can help reduce stress by promoting relaxation and mindfulness.

Physical Activity: Regular exercise not only benefits your physical health but also releases endorphins, which are natural stress relievers.

Healthy Diet: Nutrient-rich foods can support your body in dealing with stress. Avoiding excessive caffeine, sugar, and processed foods can also help stabilize your mood.

Sleep and Mental Health

Quality sleep is essential for both physical and mental health. Lack of sleep can lead to mood disorders, increased stress, and impaired cognitive function. On the flip side, mental health challenges can disrupt sleep patterns.

Sleep Hygiene: Establishing a bedtime routine and creating a sleep-conducive environment can improve sleep quality.

Stress Management: Managing stress and anxiety can significantly impact your ability to fall asleep and stay asleep.

Physical Activity: Regular exercise can promote better sleep patterns by helping your body regulate its internal clock.

Emotional Well-Being and Physical Health

Positive emotional well-being is linked to better physical health outcomes. People who experience emotional well-being tend to have healthier lifestyles, make better dietary choices, and engage in regular exercise.

Mindfulness Practices: Techniques like gratitude journaling, mindfulness meditation, and positive affirmations can foster emotional well-being.

Social Connections: Maintaining healthy relationships and strong social connections can provide emotional support and reduce the risk of depression.

Stress Reduction: Reducing chronic stress and managing negative emotions can have a positive impact on physical health.

Fitness Habits

Physical fitness is a cornerstone of health and well-being. Regular exercise offers a wide range of physical and mental benefits, making it a non-negotiable habit for a healthy life.

The Benefits of Exercise

Physical Health: Regular exercise can improve cardiovascular health, lower blood pressure, reduce the risk of chronic diseases (like heart disease and diabetes), and promote a healthy weight.

Mental Health: Exercise is a natural mood booster. It releases endorphins, reduces stress, anxiety, and depression, and enhances cognitive function.

Energy and Vitality: Physical activity increases energy levels and overall vitality. It can help you feel more alert and productive throughout the day.

Longevity: Regular exercise is associated with a longer lifespan. It promotes healthy aging by maintaining muscle mass and bone density.

Types of Exercise

There are various types of exercise, each with its unique benefits. A well-rounded fitness routine often includes a combination of the following:

Cardiovascular (Aerobic) Exercise: Activities like jogging, cycling, swimming, and dancing improve cardiovascular health, burn calories, and boost endurance.

Strength Training: Resistance training, using weights or bodyweight exercises, helps build muscle mass, improve metabolism, and enhance functional strength.

Flexibility and Mobility Training: Practices like yoga and stretching routines improve flexibility, posture, and overall mobility.

Mind-Body Exercises: Activities like tai chi and Pilates combine physical movement with mindfulness, promoting balance and stress reduction.

Building an Exercise Habit

Starting and maintaining an exercise habit can be challenging, but it's incredibly rewarding. Here are steps to help you build and sustain this essential habit:

Set Clear Goals: Define your fitness goals, whether they involve weight loss, strength gain, improved endurance, or stress reduction. Having clear objectives will motivate you.

Start Slow: If you're new to exercise, begin with manageable activities and gradually increase intensity and duration. This reduces the risk of injury and burnout.

Find Enjoyment: Choose activities you enjoy. Exercise should be something you look forward to, not a chore. Trying various activities can help you discover what you like.

Create a Routine: Consistency is key. Schedule your workouts at specific times, making them a regular part of your day.

Find Accountability: Exercise with a friend, join a fitness class, or hire a personal trainer. Accountability can boost motivation and commitment.

Track Your Progress: Keep a fitness journal or use a fitness app to monitor your workouts and celebrate your achievements.

Be Patient: Results may not be immediate, but with time and consistency, you'll see improvements in your physical and mental well-being.

Nutrition Habits

Nutrition plays a vital role in overall health and well-being. What you eat directly impacts your energy levels, immune function, and long-term health. Developing healthy eating habits is an investment in your future well-being.

The Benefits of Healthy Eating

Physical Health: A balanced diet supports healthy growth, maintenance of body weight, and reduces the risk of chronic diseases, including heart disease, diabetes, and certain cancers.

Mental Health: Nutrition can impact mood and cognitive function. A diet rich in nutrients supports brain health and emotional well-being.

Energy and Focus: Eating the right foods provides a steady source of energy, helps maintain blood sugar levels, and enhances concentration.

Digestive Health: A diet high in fiber and nutrient-rich foods supports a healthy digestive system, reducing the risk of gastrointestinal issues.

Elements of a Healthy Diet

A healthy diet is characterized by the following key elements:

Variety: Eating a wide range of foods ensures you receive a broad spectrum of nutrients. Aim to include fruits, vegetables, whole grains, lean proteins, and healthy fats in your diet.

Portion Control: Be mindful of portion sizes to avoid overeating. Pay attention to hunger and fullness cues.

Balanced Macronutrients: A balanced diet includes an appropriate balance of carbohydrates, proteins, and fats. Choose complex carbohydrates, lean proteins, and healthy fats.

Hydration: Proper hydration is essential for bodily functions. Aim to drink plenty of water throughout the day.

Moderation: It's okay to enjoy occasional treats and indulgences, but they should be consumed in moderation.

Building Healthy Eating Habits

Creating and maintaining healthy eating habits can be challenging in a world filled with convenience foods and tempting treats. However, it's entirely possible with the right approach:

Educate Yourself: Learn about nutrition and understand the importance of different nutrients in your diet. Knowledge empowers you to make informed choices.

Plan Your Meals: Meal planning helps you make healthy choices and reduces the temptation of fast food or unhealthy snacks.

Cook at Home: Preparing meals at home allows you to control ingredients and portion sizes. It can also be a fun and rewarding activity.

Mindful Eating: Pay attention to what you eat and savor each bite. Mindful eating can help you enjoy your meals and prevent overeating.

Listen to Your Body: Tune into your body's hunger and fullness cues. Avoid eating out of boredom or stress.

Avoid Emotional Eating: Find alternative ways to cope with emotions, such as stress or boredom, instead of turning to food.

Seek Professional Guidance: If you have specific dietary needs or health concerns, consult a registered dietitian or nutritionist for personalized guidance.

Stress Management Habits

Stress is a ubiquitous part of modern life, but chronic stress can take a toll on your physical and mental health. Effective stress management habits are crucial for maintaining well-being.

The Impact of Stress

Chronic stress is associated with various health issues, including:

Cardiovascular Problems: Stress can lead to high blood pressure, heart disease, and an increased risk of heart attacks.

Weakened Immune System: Prolonged stress can suppress the immune system, making you more susceptible to illnesses.

Mental Health Challenges: Stress is a significant contributor to anxiety and depression.

Digestive Issues: Stress can exacerbate gastrointestinal problems, such as irritable bowel syndrome (IBS).

Sleep Disturbances: Stress often disrupts sleep patterns, leading to insomnia or poor sleep quality.

Stress Management Techniques

Effective stress management involves adopting techniques and habits that help you cope with and reduce stress. Here are some valuable stress management practices:

Mindfulness Meditation: Mindfulness involves paying attention to the present moment without judgment. Meditation and mindfulness exercises can reduce stress and promote emotional well-being.

Deep Breathing Exercises: Practicing deep breathing techniques can help calm your nervous system and reduce stress levels.

Physical Activity: Regular exercise is a natural stress reliever. It releases endorphins and helps you manage stress more effectively.

Time Management: Effective time management can reduce feelings of overwhelm and help you regain a sense of control.

Healthy Boundaries: Setting boundaries in your personal and professional life can prevent burnout and reduce stress.

Social Support: Maintaining healthy relationships and seeking support from friends and loved ones can provide emotional relief during stressful times.

Creative Outlets: Engaging in creative activities like art, music, or writing can be therapeutic and reduce stress.

Positive Affirmations: Use positive affirmations to counter negative thoughts and promote a positive mindset.

Professional Help: If stress becomes overwhelming, consider seeking support from a mental health professional or counselor.

Sleep Hygiene Habits

Quality sleep is essential for overall health and well-being. Poor sleep can impact your mood, cognitive function, and physical health. Developing good sleep hygiene habits can improve the quality and duration of your sleep.

The Importance of Sleep

Physical Health: Adequate sleep supports immune function, cardiovascular health, and hormone regulation. It aids in muscle recovery and repair.

Mental Health: Sleep is crucial for emotional regulation and cognitive function. Poor sleep can lead to mood disturbances, anxiety, and depression.

Productivity: A well-rested mind is more alert, focused, and productive. Quality sleep enhances cognitive performance and problem-solving abilities.

Energy Levels: Quality sleep helps maintain energy levels throughout the day, reducing fatigue and irritability.

Longevity: Chronic sleep deprivation is associated with a higher risk of mortality. Quality sleep contributes to a longer and healthier life.

Creating a Sleep-Inducing Environment

Improving your sleep quality begins with creating a sleep-conducive environment:

Comfortable Bed: Invest in a comfortable mattress and pillows that provide adequate support.

Darkness: Keep your bedroom dark and eliminate sources of light that may disrupt your sleep.

Cool Temperature: A cooler room temperature is generally more conducive to sleep.

Quietness: Minimize noise disturbances in your sleep environment. Earplugs or white noise machines can be helpful.

Limit Screen Time: Avoid screens (phones, tablets, computers, TVs) at least an hour before bedtime, as the blue light emitted can interfere with sleep.

Sleep Routine and Schedule

Establishing a consistent sleep routine and schedule can improve sleep quality:

Regular Bedtime: Go to bed and wake up at the same time every day, even on weekends.

Bedtime Routine: Develop a calming bedtime routine to signal to your body that it's time to wind down. Activities like reading, gentle stretching, or relaxation exercises can be included.

Limit Naps: If you take daytime naps, keep them short (20-30 minutes) and earlier in the day to avoid interfering with nighttime sleep.

Avoid Stimulants: Reduce or eliminate caffeine and nicotine intake, especially in the hours leading up to bedtime.

Limit Fluids: Reduce the consumption of fluids close to bedtime to minimize nighttime awakenings for bathroom trips.

Case Study: Maria's Journey to Well-Being

To illustrate the power of health and wellness habits, let's explore Maria's story. Maria, a busy professional and mother, was struggling to balance work, family, and personal well-being.

Maria's Challenge: Maria often felt overwhelmed and fatigued. She lacked energy for her family and felt she was neglecting her health.

Health and Wellness Transformation: Maria recognized the need for change and began cultivating health and wellness habits:

- **Exercise Routine:** Maria incorporated regular walks and home workouts into her daily routine. This physical activity boosted her energy levels and reduced stress.

- **Balanced Nutrition:** She started planning nutritious meals and prioritizing fruits, vegetables, and whole grains. This change provided her with sustained energy throughout the day.

- Stress Management: Maria began practicing mindfulness meditation and deep breathing exercises to manage stress. These techniques helped her stay calm and focused.

- Improved Sleep Hygiene: Maria established a consistent sleep schedule and created a sleep-conducive environment in her bedroom. Her quality of sleep improved significantly.

Transformation: Over time, these health and wellness habits had a remarkable impact on Maria's life. She had more energy to engage with her family, excelled at work, and felt a deep sense of well-being. Her journey demonstrates that even small changes in health habits can lead to significant improvements in overall quality of life.

<u>Key Takeaways</u>

- The mind-body connection underscores the importance of holistic self-care for physical and mental well-being.

- Fitness habits promote physical health, mental well-being, energy, and longevity.

- Healthy eating habits provide essential nutrients for overall health, energy, and mood.

- Stress management habits are crucial for reducing chronic stress and maintaining emotional well-being.

- Sleep hygiene habits improve the quality and duration of sleep, impacting physical and mental health.

9

Relationship and Communication Habits

Introduction: The Building Blocks of Connection

Our relationships with others are among the most significant aspects of our lives. In this chapter, we'll explore the habits that foster positive relationships, effective communication, and emotional intelligence. Whether you're aiming to strengthen your personal bonds or enhance your professional connections, the habits discussed here will empower you to build meaningful and fulfilling relationships.

The Importance of Relationships

Strong and healthy relationships are essential for our overall well-being and happiness. Whether it's our relationships with family, friends, colleagues, or romantic partners, they shape our lives in profound ways.

Why Relationships Matter

Emotional Support: Relationships provide us with emotional support during challenging times, reducing stress and anxiety.

Personal Growth: Interacting with others exposes us to different perspectives and experiences, promoting personal growth and empathy.

Happiness: Positive relationships are a significant predictor of happiness and life satisfaction.

Professional Success: Strong professional relationships are essential for career growth and job satisfaction.

Longevity: Studies show that individuals with strong social connections tend to live longer, healthier lives.

Habits for Building Positive Relationships

Building and maintaining positive relationships require intentional habits that nurture trust, understanding, and connection.

Active Listening

Empathetic Listening: Practice empathetic listening by genuinely trying to understand the other person's perspective and emotions.

Avoid Interrupting: Resist the urge to interrupt or offer solutions prematurely. Let the other person express themselves fully.

Ask Open-Ended Questions: Encourage meaningful conversation by asking open-ended questions that invite discussion and reflection.

Effective Communication

Clear and Honest Communication: Be clear and honest in your communication, expressing your thoughts and feelings openly.

Constructive Feedback: When offering feedback, focus on constructive criticism that helps the other person grow and improve.

Respectful Communication: Maintain respect and courtesy in all your interactions, even during disagreements.

Empathy and Understanding

Put Yourself in Their Shoes: Try to see situations from the other person's perspective. Empathizing with their feelings and experiences strengthens your connection.

Validate Emotions: Acknowledge and validate the other person's emotions, even if you don't necessarily agree with their viewpoint.

Practice Patience: Be patient and understanding, especially when the other person is going through difficult times.

Quality Time

Prioritize Quality Time: Dedicate quality time to spend with loved ones, free from distractions like phones or work.

Quality Over Quantity: It's not about the quantity of time spent together but the quality of your interactions that matters most.

Shared Activities: Engage in activities you both enjoy, as shared experiences can deepen your connection.

Emotional Intelligence Habits

Emotional intelligence is the ability to recognize, understand, manage, and use emotions effectively in both yourself and others. Cultivating emotional intelligence is crucial for building and maintaining healthy relationships.

Self-Awareness

Self-Reflection: Take time to reflect on your emotions, triggers, and reactions. Self-awareness is the foundation of emotional intelligence.

Identify Your Emotions: Practice identifying and labeling your emotions accurately.

Journaling: Keep a journal to track your emotional experiences and patterns over time.

Self-Regulation

Emotion Regulation: Develop strategies to manage your emotions constructively, such as deep breathing, meditation, or mindfulness.

Impulse Control: Work on controlling impulsive reactions and taking a step back to respond thoughtfully.

Conflict Resolution Skills: Learn effective conflict resolution techniques to handle disagreements calmly and productively.

Empathy

Practice Perspective-Taking: Train yourself to see situations from others' viewpoints, understanding their emotions and needs.

Active Listening: Employ active listening skills to show that you genuinely care about the other person's feelings and thoughts.

Cultural Sensitivity: Be aware of cultural differences and how they may impact emotions and communication.

Social Skills

Communication Skills: Enhance your communication skills, including non-verbal cues, active listening, and assertiveness.

Conflict Resolution: Develop skills for resolving conflicts and handling difficult conversations with empathy and diplomacy.

Networking: Build and maintain a strong professional network through effective social interactions.

Conflict Resolution Habits

Conflict is a natural part of any relationship, but how we handle it can make or break the connection. Healthy conflict resolution habits are essential for maintaining positive relationships.

Open Communication

Encourage Openness: Create an environment where both parties feel comfortable expressing their concerns and feelings.

Active Listening: Listen actively and attentively to the other person's perspective, showing that you value their viewpoint.

Avoid Blame and Criticism: Focus on the issue at hand rather than assigning blame or criticizing the other person's character.

Empathy and Understanding

Empathize with Their Perspective: Try to understand the other person's viewpoint and emotions, even if you disagree.

Use "I" Statements: Express your feelings and needs using "I" statements, which are less accusatory and more constructive.

Ask for Clarification: If something is unclear, ask for clarification to ensure you fully grasp the other person's perspective.

Problem-Solving

Collaborative Approach: Approach conflict as a problem to solve together, rather than a battle to win.

Brainstorm Solutions: Work together to generate potential solutions that address both parties' needs.

Negotiation Skills: Learn negotiation techniques to find mutually beneficial compromises.

Relationship Maintenance Habits

Maintaining healthy relationships requires ongoing effort and commitment. These habits help nurture and strengthen your connections over time.

Quality Time

Scheduled Dates: Set aside regular, dedicated time for dates or outings with your partner or loved ones.

Unplugged Time: Disconnect from digital devices during quality time to ensure you're fully present.

Variety: Keep your relationship fresh by trying new activities and experiences together.

Gratitude and Appreciation

Express Gratitude: Regularly express appreciation for your loved ones and the positive aspects of your relationship.

Surprise Gestures: Surprise your partner or loved ones with small, thoughtful gestures to show your affection.

Celebrate Milestones: Celebrate special occasions and milestones to commemorate your journey together.

Communication

Check-Ins: Have regular check-in conversations to discuss your relationship, goals, and any concerns or needs.

Conflict Resolution: Address conflicts promptly and constructively rather than letting them fester.

Affectionate Communication: Maintain affectionate and loving communication to reinforce your bond.

Case Study: Sarah and Michael's Journey to Relationship Bliss

To illustrate the power of relationship and communication habits, let's explore the story of Sarah and Michael, a married couple facing common relationship challenges.

Sarah and Michael's Challenge: Over time, Sarah and Michael's communication had deteriorated, leading to misunderstandings and occasional conflicts.

Relationship and Communication Transformation: Recognizing the need for change, Sarah and Michael began implementing relationship and communication habits:

- **Active Listening:** They learned to listen actively to each other's perspectives, even when they disagreed.

- **Empathy:** Both Sarah and Michael made an effort to empathize with each other's feelings and experiences.

- **Scheduled Quality Time:** They established a weekly date night to prioritize quality time together.

- **Conflict Resolution Skills:** Sarah and Michael worked on constructive conflict resolution techniques, focusing on finding solutions rather than assigning blame.

Transformation: Over time, these relationship and communication habits had a transformative impact on Sarah and Michael's marriage. They communicated more openly, understood each other better, and strengthened their bond, leading to a more fulfilling and harmonious relationship.

Key Takeaways

- Positive relationships are crucial for well-being, personal growth, and happiness.

- Relationship-building habits involve active listening, effective communication, empathy, and quality time.

- Emotional intelligence habits enhance self-awareness, self-regulation, empathy, and social skills.

- Conflict resolution habits promote healthy conflict resolution and problem-solving.

- Relationship maintenance habits include quality time, gratitude, and ongoing communication.

10

Financial and Wealth-Building Habits

Introduction: The Path to Financial Prosperity

Financial well-being is a cornerstone of a fulfilling life. In this chapter, we'll explore the habits that promote financial stability, responsible money management, and wealth-building. Whether you're looking to improve your financial situation, save for the future, or achieve financial independence, the habits discussed here will empower you to take control of your finances and pave the way for a secure and prosperous future.

The Significance of Financial Well-Being

Financial well-being extends beyond having enough money to cover expenses. It encompasses financial security, freedom, and the ability to pursue your life goals.

Why Financial Well-Being Matters

Freedom and Choices: Financial well-being provides you with the freedom to make choices that align with your values and aspirations.

Peace of Mind: It reduces financial stress and anxiety, allowing you to enjoy greater peace of mind.

Achieving Goals: Financial stability is essential for achieving life goals, whether it's homeownership, travel, education, or retirement.

Emergency Preparedness: It ensures you're prepared for unexpected expenses and emergencies without going into debt.

Generational Impact: Responsible financial habits can positively impact future generations by passing on financial knowledge and stability.

Habits for Financial Stability

Financial stability is built upon a foundation of responsible money management and smart financial decisions.

Budgeting

Create a Budget: Develop a comprehensive budget that tracks your income, expenses, and savings goals.

Track Expenses: Keep a record of all your expenses to gain insight into your spending patterns.

Review Regularly: Periodically review and adjust your budget to ensure it aligns with your financial goals.

Saving and Emergency Funds

Automate Savings: Set up automatic transfers to savings accounts to ensure consistent saving.

Emergency Fund: Establish an emergency fund with three to six months' worth of living expenses to cover unexpected costs.

Savings Goals: Set specific savings goals, whether it's for a vacation, a home purchase, or retirement.

Debt Management

Debt Reduction Plan: Develop a plan to pay off existing debts, prioritizing high-interest debts first.

Responsible Credit Use: Use credit responsibly, avoiding excessive credit card debt and paying bills on time.

Credit Score Monitoring: Regularly monitor your credit score and take steps to improve it if necessary.

Wealth-Building Habits

Building wealth goes beyond financial stability. It involves strategic actions to accumulate assets and investments over time.

Investment Strategy

Invest Wisely: Develop an investment strategy that aligns with your financial goals, risk tolerance, and time horizon.

Diversification: Diversify your investment portfolio to spread risk and increase potential returns.

Regular Contributions: Consistently contribute to your investments, such as retirement accounts or brokerage accounts.

Retirement Planning

Set Retirement Goals: Define your retirement goals and the lifestyle you want to maintain in retirement.

Start Early: The earlier you start saving for retirement, the more time your investments have to grow.

Maximize Retirement Accounts: Contribute the maximum allowable amount to retirement accounts like 401(k)s or IRAs.

Passive Income Streams

Real Estate Investments: Explore real estate investments, such as rental properties or real estate investment trusts (REITs).

Dividend Stocks: Invest in dividend-paying stocks or funds to generate passive income.

Side Hustles: Develop side businesses or freelance work to generate additional income streams.

Financial Education and Literacy

Financial literacy is the cornerstone of effective financial management. Cultivating financial education habits empowers you to make informed financial decisions.

Self-Education

Read Financial Literature: Explore books, articles, and courses on personal finance and investment.

Stay Informed: Keep up-to-date with financial news and trends that may impact your financial decisions.

Attend Workshops and Seminars: Participate in financial workshops or seminars to expand your knowledge.

Seek Professional Guidance

Financial Advisor: Consider consulting with a financial advisor to develop a comprehensive financial plan.

Tax Advisor: Seek advice from a tax professional to optimize your tax strategy.

Estate Planning: Consult an estate planning attorney to ensure your financial assets are distributed according to your wishes.

Frugal Living

Frugality involves mindful spending and resourcefulness to make the most of your income.

Mindful Spending

Prioritize Needs Over Wants: Distinguish between essential expenses and discretionary spending.

Comparison Shopping: Comparison shop to find the best deals and discounts on purchases.

Limit Impulse Buys: Avoid impulse buying by implementing a cooling-off period before making non-essential purchases.

Resourcefulness

DIY Projects: Consider do-it-yourself (DIY) projects for home maintenance or repairs.

Minimalism: Embrace minimalism by decluttering and simplifying your possessions and lifestyle.

Energy Efficiency: Implement energy-efficient practices to reduce utility bills.

Charitable Giving

Giving back to others and contributing to causes you care about is a meaningful aspect of financial well-being.

Charitable Budgeting

Allocate Funds: Set aside a portion of your income specifically for charitable giving.

Research Charities: Research and vet charitable organizations to ensure your contributions are used effectively.

Regular Donations: Make regular donations to your chosen charities to support their missions consistently.

Financial Communication

Effective communication about finances is crucial, especially in relationships or partnerships.

Open Dialogue

Financial Transparency: Maintain open and transparent communication with your partner or family members about financial matters.

Joint Goals: Collaboratively set financial goals and create a financial plan that aligns with shared aspirations.

Regular Financial Meetings: Schedule regular meetings to review financial progress and make adjustments as needed.

Teach Financial Literacy

Family Education: Educate your children or family members about financial literacy and responsible money management.

Lead by Example: Be a role model for responsible financial behavior, demonstrating the importance of saving, budgeting, and investing.

Encourage Questions: Encourage questions and discussions about finances to promote financial literacy within your family.

Case Study: Emily's Journey to Financial Independence

To illustrate the power of financial and wealth-building habits, let's explore Emily's story. Emily, a young professional, aspired to achieve financial independence and retire early.

Emily's Challenge: Emily faced significant student loan debt and was determined to become financially independent.

Financial Independence Transformation: Recognizing the need for change, Emily embraced financial and wealth-building habits:

- **Budgeting:** She created a strict budget, allowing her to pay off her student loans ahead of schedule.

- **Investment Strategy:** Emily developed a diversified investment portfolio, focusing on long-term wealth accumulation.

- **Frugal Living:** She adopted a frugal lifestyle, making mindful spending decisions and prioritizing savings.

- **Side Hustle:** Emily started a successful side business that generated additional income.

Transformation: Over time, these financial and wealth-building habits enabled Emily to pay off her student loans, accumulate substantial savings, and achieve her dream of early retirement. Her journey demonstrates that intentional financial habits can lead to financial independence and the freedom to pursue one's passions.

Key Takeaways

- Financial well-being encompasses financial stability, responsible money management, and wealth-building.

- Habits for financial stability include budgeting, saving, debt management, and responsible credit use.

- Wealth-building habits involve strategic investments, retirement planning, passive income streams, and financial education.

- Frugality and charitable giving contribute to effective financial management.

- Open financial communication and teaching financial literacy promote responsible financial behavior.

11

Habit Mastery and Sustaining Positive Change

Introduction: The Journey of Lasting Transformation

Congratulations on your journey thus far. In this chapter, we'll delve into the art of habit mastery and sustaining positive change. You've learned how to build good habits and break bad ones, but now it's time to ensure that these changes endure and become a seamless part of your life. Whether you seek to master your habits for personal growth, career success, or overall well-being, the insights and strategies discussed here will empower you to maintain the positive changes you've worked so hard to achieve.

The Challenge of Habit Relapse

Maintaining positive changes can be challenging. Many individuals who successfully build new habits experience setbacks or relapses. Understanding the common challenges can help you stay on track.

Common Challenges

Complacency: After initial success, it's easy to become complacent and revert to old habits.

Stress and Triggers: Stressful situations or familiar triggers can lead to the reemergence of bad habits.

Overconfidence: Feeling overly confident about your ability to maintain a habit can lead to neglect and eventual relapse.

Life Changes: Significant life changes, such as a new job or family responsibilities, can disrupt established routines.

Lack of Adaptability: Failing to adapt to changing circumstances can undermine habit maintenance.

Habit Mastery: Going Beyond Initial Success

Habit mastery involves moving beyond the initial stages of habit formation and achieving a level where the behavior becomes almost second nature.

Consistency

Daily Practice: Maintain consistent daily practice of the habit to reinforce it.

Routine Integration: Incorporate the habit seamlessly into your daily routine so that it becomes an automatic part of your day.

Time and Patience: Understand that habit mastery takes time and patience. Be prepared for the long haul.

Monitoring and Feedback

Self-Reflection: Regularly reflect on your progress and identify areas for improvement.

Feedback Loop: Seek feedback from accountability partners, mentors, or coaches to refine your habits.

Adjustment: Be open to adjusting your habit as needed to better align with your goals and lifestyle.

Deepening the Habit

Skill Development: Focus on improving and mastering the skills associated with your habit.

Advanced Techniques: Explore advanced techniques or variations of the habit to keep it fresh and engaging.

Challenge Yourself: Set higher benchmarks and challenges related to the habit to continue pushing your limits.

Sustaining Positive Change

Maintaining positive changes involves strategies that go beyond habit mastery and address the long-term sustainability of those changes.

Integration into Identity

Identity Shift: Embrace the habit as part of your identity. When it aligns with who you are, it becomes easier to maintain.

Values Alignment: Ensure that the habit aligns with your core values, making it more meaningful and sustainable.

Internal Motivation: Shift from external motivations (e.g., rewards) to internal motivations (e.g., intrinsic satisfaction).

Accountability and Support

Maintain Accountability: Continue to be accountable to yourself or others for the habit.

Support Network: Lean on your support network during challenging times.

Peer Groups: Engage in peer groups or communities that share your habit or goal.

Reflection and Adaptation

Regular Review: Periodically review your habit and its impact on your life.

Adapt to Changes: Adjust the habit to accommodate changes in your circumstances or priorities.

Continuous Learning: Keep learning about your habit and its nuances to stay engaged.

Overcoming Setbacks and Relapses

Setbacks and relapses are a natural part of habit formation and maintenance. What matters is how you respond to them.

Resilience

Resilient Mindset: Cultivate a resilient mindset that views setbacks as opportunities for growth.

Learn from Failure: Analyze setbacks to understand their causes and apply those lessons to future efforts.

Recommit: If you falter, recommit to your habit and restart with determination.

Recovery Strategies

Back on Track Plan: Develop a plan for getting back on track when you experience a setback.

Immediate Action: Take immediate action to address the issue and regain momentum.

Seek Support: Reach out to your support network for encouragement and assistance.

Case Study: Sarah's Journey to Habit Mastery

Let's explore Sarah's story to illustrate the process of habit mastery and sustaining positive change. Sarah had successfully built the habit of daily exercise but wanted to take it to the next level.

Sarah's Challenge: Sarah faced the challenge of plateauing in her fitness progress and wanted to deepen her exercise habit.

Habit Mastery Transformation: Recognizing the need for growth, Sarah pursued habit mastery by implementing several strategies:

- **Consistency:** She committed to daily exercise without exceptions, even on challenging days.

- **Monitoring and Feedback:** Sarah tracked her progress, sought guidance from a fitness coach, and adjusted her workout routines.

- **Deepening the Habit:** She began exploring advanced fitness techniques and set performance goals beyond her previous achievements.

Sustaining Positive Change: To sustain her positive change, Sarah integrated her exercise habit into her identity as a fitness enthusiast. She aligned it with her core value of health and continued to challenge herself with new fitness goals.

Overcoming Setbacks: When Sarah experienced setbacks, such as injury or illness, she maintained her resilient mindset, learned from the experience, and adapted her exercise routine accordingly.

Transformation: Through her commitment to habit mastery and sustaining positive change, Sarah achieved significant progress in her fitness journey and maintained a healthy lifestyle over the long term.

Key Takeaways

- Habit mastery involves achieving a high level of proficiency and consistency in your habit.

- Sustaining positive change requires integrating the habit into your identity, aligning it with your values, and maintaining internal motivation.

- Overcoming setbacks and relapses is crucial for long-term habit maintenance.

- Resilience, recovery strategies, and continuous adaptation are essential for sustaining positive changes.

12

Overcoming Common Obstacles

Introduction: The Road to Resilience

As you journey toward reshaping your habits and building a more fulfilling life, you'll inevitably encounter obstacles along the way. This chapter is dedicated to helping you identify, navigate, and conquer the common challenges that can hinder your progress. Whether it's dealing with self-doubt, managing time effectively, or handling unexpected setbacks, the insights and strategies discussed here will empower you to build resilience and maintain momentum on your path to success.

The Nature of Obstacles

Obstacles are a natural part of any transformative journey. They can manifest in various forms, both internal and external, and present unique challenges to overcome. Recognizing the nature of these obstacles is the first step in addressing them effectively.

Internal Obstacles

Self-Doubt: Doubting your abilities or the feasibility of your goals can erode your confidence.

Procrastination: Delaying tasks or putting off habit-building efforts can hinder progress.

Lack of Motivation: A lack of enthusiasm or motivation can lead to inertia and inaction.

Fear of Failure: The fear of failing or making mistakes can paralyze decision-making and risk-taking.

External Obstacles

Time Constraints: A busy schedule or lack of time management can impede your ability to focus on building habits.

Resource Limitations: Limited access to resources or support can hinder your efforts.

Negative Influences: Surrounding yourself with unsupportive or discouraging individuals can create headwinds.

Unforeseen Circumstances: Life is unpredictable, and unexpected events can disrupt your routines and plans.

Strategies for Overcoming Obstacles

Overcoming obstacles requires a combination of self-awareness, resilience, and strategic thinking. Here are effective strategies for addressing common obstacles on your journey to reshaping your habits and life.

Self-Awareness

Identify Obstacles: Recognize and acknowledge the specific obstacles that are hindering your progress.

Understand Triggers: Explore the triggers or underlying causes of your internal obstacles, such as self-doubt or procrastination.

Mindfulness: Practice mindfulness to increase awareness of your thoughts, emotions, and reactions in the face of obstacles.

Resilience

Develop Resilience: Cultivate resilience by viewing obstacles as opportunities for growth and learning.

Positive Mindset: Adopt a positive mindset that focuses on solutions rather than dwelling on problems.

Self-Compassion: Be kind to yourself when you encounter setbacks or challenges. Avoid self-criticism.

Strategic Planning

Goal Refinement: Refine and clarify your goals to ensure they align with your values and priorities.

Prioritization: Prioritize your goals and habits to allocate your time and resources effectively.

Actionable Steps: Break down your goals into actionable, manageable steps to make progress more achievable.

Time Management

Time Blocking: Implement time-blocking techniques to allocate specific time slots for habit-building activities.

Eliminate Time Wasters: Identify and eliminate time-wasting activities or distractions that hinder your productivity.

Consistency: Prioritize consistency in your routines and habits to build momentum over time.

Support and Accountability

Accountability Partner: Partner with a friend, family member, or mentor who can hold you accountable for your goals and habits.

Support Network: Surround yourself with a supportive network of individuals who encourage your progress.

Seek Help: Don't hesitate to seek professional help or guidance when faced with complex obstacles.

Adaptation

Flexibility: Embrace flexibility in your plans and strategies to adapt to changing circumstances.

Learn from Setbacks: Analyze setbacks as opportunities for learning and growth. Apply lessons to future efforts.

Resourcefulness: Develop resourcefulness by seeking creative solutions to obstacles when resources are limited.

Case Study: Jake's Journey to Overcoming Self-Doubt

Let's explore Jake's story to illustrate how one can overcome internal obstacles, such as self-doubt, on the path to habit reshaping and personal growth.

Jake's Challenge: Jake had a persistent habit of self-doubt that often prevented him from pursuing his goals.

Overcoming Self-Doubt Transformation: Recognizing the need for change, Jake embarked on a journey to overcome self-doubt by implementing several strategies:

- **Self-Awareness:** He identified specific triggers for his self-doubt, such as comparing himself to others.

- **Resilience:** Jake cultivated resilience by viewing self-doubt as an opportunity to learn and grow.

- **Positive Mindset:** He adopted a positive mindset by reframing negative thoughts and focusing on his strengths.

- **Strategic Planning:** Jake refined his goals and prioritized them to align with his values.

- **Time Management:** He implemented time-blocking techniques to dedicate focused time to his goals.

- **Support Network:** Jake sought support from a close friend who provided encouragement and accountability.

Transformation: Over time, Jake's dedication to overcoming self-doubt allowed him to build resilience and confidence. He made significant progress in reshaping his habits and achieving his goals.

Key Takeaways

- Obstacles are a natural part of any transformative journey, manifesting as internal and external challenges.

- Effective strategies for overcoming obstacles include self-awareness, resilience, strategic planning, time management, support and accountability, and adaptation.

- Viewing obstacles as opportunities for growth and learning is key to building resilience and maintaining progress.

POSTFACE

Celebrating Your Transformative Journey

Congratulations on completing this remarkable journey of personal growth and habit transformation. As we conclude this book, it's an opportunity to reflect on your achievements, revisit key insights, and prepare for the inspiring path that lies ahead.

Reflecting on Your Transformational Journey

Your journey through this book has been a profound exploration of the power of habits and their influence on your life. As we conclude, let's take a moment to review and appreciate the critical elements of this transformative process:

Understanding Habits

- **The Habit Loop:** You've gained insights into how the habit loop of cue, routine, and reward shapes your behavior.

- **Keystone Habits:** You've discovered the significance of keystone habits, which have a ripple effect on other areas of your life.

- **Habit Formation:** You've explored the science of habit formation, from identifying cues to reinforcing rewards.

Building Good Habits

- **Goal Setting:** You've learned the art of setting clear, SMART goals and their role in habit-building.

- **Consistency:** You've understood the power of daily practice and routine in building good habits.

- **Motivation and Rewards:** You've explored various motivation strategies and rewards to strengthen positive behavior.

Breaking Bad Habits

- **Identifying Triggers:** You've practiced recognizing the triggers that lead to bad habits and developed strategies for intervention.

- **Substitution:** You've discovered the concept of habit substitution, effectively replacing bad habits with healthier alternatives.

- **Accountability:** You've seen the importance of accountability, whether through self-accountability or external support, in breaking bad habits.

Habit Mastery and Sustainability

- **Mastery:** You've learned the path to habit mastery, where behaviors become second nature.

- **Sustaining Positive Change:** You've embraced the challenge of integrating positive changes into your identity and aligning them with your values.

- **Overcoming Setbacks:** You've gained resilience and strategies for overcoming setbacks and relapses on your journey.

Gratitude and Positivity

- **Gratitude Habit:** You've embraced the practice of gratitude, fostering positivity and well-being in your life.

- **Science of Gratitude:** You've explored the scientific basis of gratitude's impact on the brain, body, and emotions.

- **Gratitude in Relationships:** You've recognized how gratitude can strengthen relationships and enhance connections with others.

Overcoming Common Obstacles

- **Self-Awareness:** You've honed your self-awareness, identifying and addressing common obstacles on your path.

- **Resilience:** You've cultivated resilience, viewing obstacles as opportunities for growth and learning.

- **Strategic Planning:** You've become adept at strategic planning and time management to navigate challenges effectively.

Charting Your Future Path

As you conclude this chapter, take a moment to consider your future course on this transformative journey. The process of building and reshaping habits is ongoing, and your path forward is uniquely your own. Here are key considerations to guide you:

Goal Refinement

- **Review Your Goals:** Revisit your goals and assess your progress. Celebrate your achievements and adjust your goals as needed.

- **New Horizons:** Consider setting new goals that align with your evolving priorities and aspirations.

Habit Integration

- **Consistency:** Maintain your habits with unwavering consistency. Keep them an integral part of your daily life.

- **Deepening Mastery:** Challenge yourself to deepen your skills and knowledge in areas where you've mastered certain habits.

Resilience and Adaptability

- **Resilience:** Continue to cultivate resilience in the face of setbacks and challenges. Use setbacks as stepping stones to greater success.

- **Adaptability:** Embrace adaptability as a core skill. Life is dynamic, and your habits may need adjustment as circumstances change.

Lifelong Learning

- **Continuous Growth:** Commit to lifelong learning and personal growth. Stay curious and open to new ideas and experiences.

- **Reading and Resources:** Explore books, articles, and resources aligned with your interests and goals. Seek mentors and communities that support your journey.

Gratitude Practice

- **Daily Gratitude:** Maintain your daily gratitude practice. It's a powerful tool for maintaining positivity and well-being.

- **Gratitude to Others:** Continue expressing gratitude to the people who support and inspire you.

Embracing Your Power to Transform

This book has provided you with a strong foundation for personal growth, resilience, and transformation through intentional habit-building. As you conclude this chapter, remember that your journey is ongoing, and the possibilities for positive change are boundless.

Embrace your power to reshape your habits, build a more fulfilling life, and achieve your dreams. Let the knowledge and insights gained in these pages be your guide as you continue to cultivate a life filled with purpose, positivity, and personal growth.

Thank you for joining me on this incredible journey. Your future is brimming with potential, and I have no doubt that you will shape it into something extraordinary.

Keep the Conversation Going

As you move forward on your journey, remember that personal growth and transformation are lifelong processes. Stay curious, keep learning, and never stop reshaping your habits and your life.

If you ever find yourself seeking guidance, motivation, or support, don't hesitate to return to these pages. This book is your companion on your journey to becoming the best version of yourself.

Remember, the power to transform your life lies within you. Embrace it, nurture it, and continue to reshape your habits in pursuit of a more fulfilling and purpose-driven life.

Thank You

I want to express my heartfelt gratitude for joining me on this transformative journey. It has been an honor to be your guide and companion on this path of growth and self-discovery.

As you conclude this book and venture into your future, know that your potential is boundless. I believe in your ability to create positive change in your life and in the lives of those around you.

Wishing you a future filled with success, fulfillment, and the joy of reshaped habits that bring you ever closer to your dreams.

9 7 9 8 8 7 4 0 6 6 2 8 4